THE SERVE AND THE
OVERHEAD SMASH

THE SERVE
AND THE
OVERHEAD
SMASH

by *Peter Schwed*

UNITED STATES TENNIS ASSOCIATION
INSTRUCTIONAL SERIES

Illustrations by George Janes

DOUBLEDAY & COMPANY, INC.
GARDEN CITY, NEW YORK
1976

Library of Congress Cataloging in Publication Data

Schwed, Peter.
    The serve and the overhead smash.

    (Instructional series)
    1. Tennis.   I. Title.   II. Series.
GV995.S357   796.34′22
ISBN 0-385-11487-7
Library of Congress Catalog Card Number 76–10521

Contents

To my dear daughter,
LAURIE

Introduction

Some years ago, four of us went out one summer afternoon to play a casual set or two of doubles. My brother, Fred, who could only be persuaded to pick up a tennis racket when there was no golf course in the vicinity, was by far the weakest player and I was the strongest, so we teamed up against the other two.

Midway in the first set, Fred and I were both up near the net and one of our opponents tossed up a fairly high, weak lob over Fred's head which, if allowed to fall unmolested, would not have landed any deeper than midcourt. That is exactly what it did, as Fred stood there and watched it go over his head. Loving brother that I was, I still felt impelled to break the rule that a doubles player should never criticize his partner during a game.

"For crying out loud, Freddy! How about getting the lead out? If you'd taken two—possibly one step back while that ball was in the air, you'd have been in a perfect position to smash it away!"

Fred, my elder by ten years, was ever an affectionate teacher of his kid brother, and the game was interrupted while he explained.

"You see, Pete, I am a finely attuned specimen. The moment—the *very moment* that lob was hit, my brain, backed by my keen competitive instinct, flashed a message that went *instantly* to my legs, feet, arms, hands, fingers, and every cell in my body. The message was: 'Turn your left shoulder to the net as you take two half-skip glides back toward the base line, and at the same time lift your left arm with extended fingers to point at the ball, for that will enable you to follow its descent more closely. Also, at the same time prepare your racket for the hit by getting your right elbow up head high, with your right wrist cocked so the racket is in the "back-scratching position." At the exact right moment, spring into the air and like the unleashing of a coiled spring, explode all your weight into the smash, meeting the ball at impact slightly in front of your body, and using a powerful wrist snap over the top of it to powder it away at an angle that no human opponent could ever reach.'

"All of that transpired like lightning, Pete, and equally instantaneously there flashed back the message from my legs, feet, arms, hands, fingers, and every cell in my body. The message was: 'Who? *Me?*'"

I tell this story to justify the approach that this book will take. On the one hand, if you are an ardent and ambitious enough tennis player to be reading it, you will want to know everything that the best tennis players and coaches have to say about executing the service and the overhead smash perfectly, and I'll try to tell you. I've had over fifty years of attending major tournaments and, in recent ones, have watched the world's best play weekly on television as well. My collection of tennis books constitutes a small library. My own performance on the courts is good enough to have won some minor tournaments, more because of having a real knowledge of the game than because of any outstanding talents. Between one qualification and another, I think my equipment to write soundly about tennis isn't at all bad, but it would be both redundant and presumptuous if I were to confine what I have to say to what other better and more professional players and coaches have already written so clearly.

So although I will indeed summarize the best instruction I have been taught, read, or learned from observation of the world's best, I am going to devote at least a substantial minority portion of this book to those of us who would say, "Who? *Me?*" when trying to learn tennis perfection. Adaptations from ideal strokes, and even sometimes unorthodox techniques and strategies, are things that ordinary club players have to fall back upon, when they don't have the physical blessings of a Wimbledon or Forest Hills tournament entrant, and that is assuredly true of most of the people who will be reading this book. The tennis courts of the world are crowded with common-looking players, who cannot and never will aspire to greatness, but who would like to become better players, and who can.

Be of good courage. As Abraham Lincoln once said: "Common-looking people are the best in the world: that is the reason the Lord makes so many of them."

P. S.

Author's Apologies

Dear Women,

I wish there were some pronoun that conveyed "he" *or* "she," but the only possibility—"it"—doesn't seem quite right. So I have used "he," "his," and "him" throughout, rather than constantly having to employ the cumbersome "his or her" locution. I might just as well have used "she" and "her" instead, and I would have done so if I were female myself.

P. S.

Dear Left-handers,

In similar fashion, the inadequacies of the English language have made me write as if all tennis players were right-handed, which is by no means the truth. One in about every six is left-handed and, in the few cases in this book where right and left hands or feet are mentioned, I regret having to ask you to substitute one for the other. If I were left-handed myself, however, I admit I wouldn't have written differently—after all there are six times as many right-handed potential book buyers as there are of you! But I am sorry.

P. S.

THE SERVE

I

Preparing to Serve

A racket has been spun and you have won the choice of electing to serve first or of taking your pick of sides of the court. If you are a good, law-abiding, un-Machiavellian tennis player, you have undoubtedly chosen to serve first, and the chances are that it was a wise decision, even though the best tennis strategist I know invariably makes his opponent make the choice. (That is your prerogative even if you win the toss.) It is his theory that the player who has heard his rival commit himself to one thing or the other is in a stronger position to arrange matters to his own advantage and can take into account factors such as wind, sun, and psychology, that the blind choice of "I'll serve first" doesn't offer. He may be right, but the overwhelming weight of tradition is against him. Ninety-nine players out of a hundred, winning the toss, elect to serve first.

All other things being equal, it's obvious why this is a good idea. (My strategist friend would say that frequently all other things are not equal, and this can include one or the other of you having an extremely ineffective and feeble serve.) But assuming you are both good players, the server always has a distinct edge, and if he keeps winning each of his early service games when he leads off as server, he puts tremendous pressure on an opponent. Even if the latter is holding his own service when it's his turn, he is constantly falling one game behind, and he comes to feel that, if he ever loses his own serve, he's a dead duck.

It has become a truism that the serve is the biggest weapon in the armory of tennis strokes, and it is certainly true that if you never lose your own service, you'll never lose a set.*

A really big serve has carried some fairly ordinary players, by world-class standards, to the heights. John Doeg in 1930 and Bob Falkenburg in 1948 did not have the well-rounded games of some of their contemporaries, but each consistently belted such powerful serves into court that their opponents very rarely could crack them. The result was that Doeg won the U.S. championships in his year, and Falkenburg won Wimbledon in his. Frank Froeling was another old-timer who went a long way primarily on this asset, and today such fine players as Roscoe Tanner and Colin Dibley pull off some startling upsets of higher-ranking players on those special days when their services are particularly hot.

A parallel can be drawn at every lesser level than the top tournament grade. Sectional and club players, college and school players, and hackers down to novices at the game, all find the superior server in their own strata a contender to be feared, no matter how indifferent the rest of his game may be. If you can't crack his serve, you're not going to be able to beat him.

* To forestall the reader who will write that you can lose a set in which you've held serve all the way, if it has to be settled by a sudden death or tie-breaker play-off, I'll concede the point. But in that case you've lost a critical service or two in the play-off, so please don't bother to write.

The best answer is to become a superior server yourself, or at least a very effective one, and this is one case when you don't have to respond, "Who? *Me?*" For while you may not have the height or strength of a Roscoe Tanner, who is reputed to be able to serve a tennis ball at speeds up to 140 miles per hour, anyone who is intent upon learning to serve well should be able to do so within his physical limits. It takes concentration and savvy, and probably hundreds and hundreds of balls and hours of lonely practice. But the service is one tennis stroke that is yours from beginning to end, with no opponent confusing things for you, and you can learn to do it well.

Let's begin.

A BASIC FACT

It has become holy gospel, in tennis instruction, that a player must keep his eyes on the ball throughout each entire point, and that he actually sees the ball make contact with his racket at the moment of impact on every stroke. That's probably a good idea to instill into a beginner's mind, whether it's true or not, for certainly one should watch the ball like a hawk when it's in play and not be intent upon other visual attractions in the court, notably one's opponent. An experienced player always senses where his rival is without really focusing on him: For the most part, peripheral vision does the trick. An occasional quick glance at him, particularly when he has sent back a high return to you, such as a lob, is permissible in order for you to see what course he's taking and whether he's exposing himself to some passing shot you may choose to counter with. But on sharp ground strokes and volley exchanges, you certainly do have to concentrate all the time on watching the ball.

However, from long years of personal experience, and an equal number of watching the best players and seeing stop-action photographs of them making shots, I'm convinced that no one *really* sees the ball contact the strings of his racket on such shots. Almost, but not quite. You see the ball right up to that point, but as you actually hit into a ground stroke you look up a fraction of a second before impact.†

Conversely, I will agree that good serving requires—nay, demands—that you watch the ball right through impact, and that if your eyes actually were fast enough to see the strings of the racket meet the ball, they would. In the serving motion as you raise your ball-tossing arm, you should lay your head back in a synchronous motion and flick your eyes up from the ball, at the moment it leaves your hand, to sight the spot where your racket will make impact with it. It's very easy to co-ordinate these movements because you control the entire operation, the ball is not coming at you at high speed, and it's the sensible and natural thing to do anyhow. But tennis players don't always do the sensible and natural thing. Which is understandable, but not forgivable in this case. Serving, more than any other stroke, is a matter of timing, and watching the ball is absolutely vital to that. Additionally, you may sometimes be able to see an actual fault

† If you want to dispute this contention, please don't take it up with your attorney. I'm not prepared to go to court about it. I did write that I myself was convinced of it, but it's only an opinion. William Jennings Bryan's opinion was that evolution was a lot of bunk.

Watch the ball all the way on the toss.

in the way you're meeting the ball, such as hitting it below the center of your strings (which tends to make a serve go up and sail out past the service box). Recognizing what causes a faulty serve should enable you to correct it.

The overhead smash is so similar in its basics that, on those shots, too, one must watch the ball all the way into impact. So as far as this specialized book is concerned, I will agree completely with what I called a gospel teaching of tennis instruction: WATCH THE BALL!

II

The Stance

The first thing to bear in mind as you approach the service line is that nobody has a clock timing you, as in a chess match.* You can take as long as you want to appraise the situation, note where the receiver is standing, and get the right "feel." Obviously, taking a really extravagant length of time before serving is rude as well as unnecessary, but it is a great mistake to hurry your serve. For one thing, your opponent has the right to get set for your serve, and if you "quick-serve" him, he can call a legitimate "let ball" on you every time. Quick-serving is a form of gamesmanship to be deplored in any event, even if the receiver stays silent and lets you get away with it.

But the real virtues of taking your proper time lie in the benefits you yourself obtain. You can relax for a moment before the big effort that goes into a serve. You can decide upon the best target spot for each serve which, if you are anything of a tactician, will vary from point to point. Best of all, you have a chance to establish and retain your regular rhythm for effective serving, for a good service is no hit-or-miss affair but a consistent flow of legs,

* The fact is that a clock actually is used now in certain professional matches to hustle along certain players who stall past endurance, normal courtesy, and what the limits of a television program want to allow. But I doubt if this practice will ever be applied to you or to me.

body, eyes, and arms that can be repeated each time you call it into play.

This is the one moment in tennis when you dictate the stroke and the pace all by yourself, and it also happens to be the stroke that can win you the most points, either outright or as the result of following up on a good serve. So make the most of it by preparing properly, and the first step is to take your time. Stand easy and relaxed, and this includes holding the handle of your racket firmly, but not in a death grip. I'll tell you why later.

Opinions vary a bit about how close you should stand to the center of the base line when serving in singles, but today practically all of the very best players stand just about as close to it as possible, which means that the left foot is placed only about a foot to the right of center when serving into the deuce court, and about the same distance to the left of center when serving into the advantage court. This is because with today's "big game," such players invariably follow each serve up toward the net and volley the return of service. Naturally, not knowing the direction that the return is going to take, a basic starting position as close to center as possible makes sense.

Follow every serve in, and volley the return? Who? Me?

Certainly, if you can, but perhaps you can't do it effectively enough for it to be a percentage tactic for you. Your speed, or condition, or possibly general ineptitude at volleying makes it a bad gamble for you to attempt to close toward the net after the first stroke, and you prefer to stay back and play a general rear-court game until opportunity enables you to come up. In that case, I think you would do better to take up your serving stance more nearly three or four feet or so away from the center point.

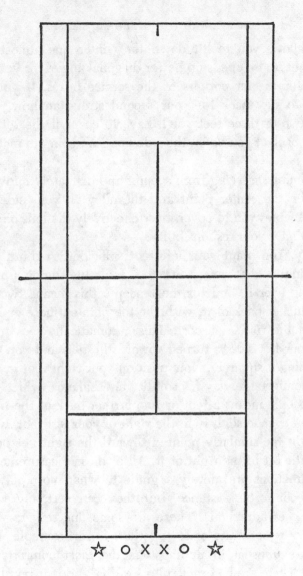

☆ ○ X X ○ ☆

X Best position for serving in singles.

○ Alternative and possibly better position for server in singles who prefers to play a rear-court game.

☆ Best position for serving in doubles.

That allows you to hit down the center line almost as well, but it also opens up better diagonal angles for you to shoot for the far corners of the service boxes. If you're going to stay back for your second stroke anyhow, the extra two or three feet you'll have to cover if the return comes back at you down the side line isn't going to matter much.

In doubles, serving from a point approximately midway between the center point and the alley on your side of court enables you to cover most effectively the half of the court that is your responsibility.

Okay. You plant your left foot sufficiently behind the base line so that you won't foot fault by edging up or jumping over it, and for most people this means two or three inches back of it, with the toe pointed more or less toward the right net post. This automatically sees to it that your left side is turned toward the net, and you are not facing it squarely. Now position your right foot in the most comfortable way for solidity and balance, which for most people means a foot or two farther back of the base line and ever so slightly to the right of your left foot, with the right toe similarly pointed toward the right net post, or a little bit to the right of it. All of these measurements and directions are merely a guide to what most players find a comfortable stance, but they can certainly vary with some individuals. There are some fine servers who keep both feet quite close together, for an example, but they are unusual in finding this the most comfortable stance. There are no exact rules for this, and it is purely a matter of "feel."

Bounce the ball once or twice before you look up, gauge your opponent's position, and go into your serve.

Bouncing the ball is a relaxing thing to do; it establishes a regular pattern and a rhythm for your serving style, and the down-and-up bounce gets you mentally prepared to stretch up and *reach* for the ball when you finally go into action.

Here is as good a place as any to say a few possibly debatable words about how many balls you should hold in your hand when serving—one or two. There is no doubt that almost all ordinary players, having committed a fault on a first serve, do not want to pause substantially before serving the second ball. They feel that the first serve, even if it has gone awry, has zeroed them in so that they can make proper corrections on the second delivery. They feel that they will lose some rhythm that the first—even if faulty—serve has established, and that they are much more likely to double-fault if there's a substantial interval between the two services. They are right. Whether it's a physical matter, or merely a mental one, most of us do have more trouble with that second ball when we've been interrupted.

So down through the years, until comparatively recently, most players held two balls in the tossing hand—which is easy to do—and served the second one, if necessary, right after committing the first fault. That is well and good if you do miss the first serve, but if that goes in, you are stuck with a ball in your hand, and either have to retain it there throughout the point or flip it out of court behind you. The one is not good, and the other is likely to be frowned upon both by court etiquette and a strict umpire. Still, short of top tournament play, where the getting rid of the second ball is certainly discouraged, that's what most of us do if we don't keep the ball in our hand. Just be sure you don't merely drop it onto the court, or fling it forward or sideways where it can be a distraction for your opponent. It's easy enough just to flip it right back of you and into the rear of your court past your base line. Do understand, however, that if your opponent objects even to that, you must hang onto the unused ball throughout the point if holding two balls is important to you on service.

Today, many players of both sexes have solved the problem by making sure that their tennis costume contains a convenient and roomy pocket. They put the second ball there, where it can be used immediately, and without breaking rhythm if the first serve goes wrong. That's probably the best solution unless, like the incredible Chris Evert, you simply don't mind breaking the flow between first and second services and can take one ball at a time from a ball boy with something close to an intermission between. Of course, Chris, with her two-handed backhand, has a particularly good reason not to want to be keeping a spare ball in her hand during play. Also, she always has a ball boy or ball girl to accommodate her, which certainly isn't true of the "Who? Me?'s" of this world.

III
Rhythm

Finding the rhythm that works best for you is a matter of practice, practice, practice. There is no practice drill more boring, but eventually more rewarding to your game, than to go out on a tennis court alone, with a boxful of old tennis balls, and practice and experiment with your serve. After you've hit a few from one side, shift and hit a few into the other service box. (Incidentally, remember to do this when you're taking practice serves before a real match. Don't just take them from the right-hand court, as so many people do. Try a few from the ad side as well.)

When you think you've got the "feel" of one type of service and it's going into court successfully, start experimenting with another until you feel equally good about that. Then start alternating different types of services, just as the best players invariably do in actual play. When you have hit all the balls you brought out with you, collect them and start all over again from the other end of the court. It is to be hoped that most of the balls will be down there in any case, for a cardinal rule of good serving is to clear the net, even if you serve too deep.

If you keep at it, you will find the rhythm pattern that works best for you. There is no absolute rule about this particular aspect of serving, for it's more a question of how one uses his body for maximum ease and power than

Work into the rhythm pattern that suits you.

it is a matter of fixed technique. Some fine servers merely poise initially with their weight slightly favoring the forward left foot, transfer it solidly back to the rear onto the right foot as they go into the backswing and toss, and then transfer forward onto the left foot completely as they swing the racket up and into impact with the ball.

Simultaneously, the right foot leaves the ground and swings forward to take the first step into court after the serve. Some equally fine servers find it effective to rock back and forth, shifting weight from one foot to the other, before finally going into the service motion in much the same manner as described above. You will see tournament players of equal distinction who have quite different patterns, one from the other, in the length of their backswings, or their arm motion on the toss. But these are all slightly varying individual styles that, in the end, aim to achieve the same result, which is to meet the toss, as the ball sits up there, with the "sweet spot" center of the racket.

Learning a serving rhythm, in which you're comfortable and have confidence, enables you to perform each of the specific techniques that are required for good serving with consistency, and consistently good serving is the name of the game. Let me never, ever serve another ace in my tennis life, but also never, ever serve a double fault,* and I'll be way ahead on the bargain, particularly when playing doubles. Yet there are many Who? Me?'s, and even good ones, who wouldn't dream of making such a deal with the Devil, for they feel that the *machismo* in whipping over an unanswerable serve now and then is worth a certain loss of consistent serving. I like such a thinker to be my opponent rather than doubles partner.

* What, *never?* Well . . . *hardly* ever!

IV

The Grip

The fact is that a person *can* clear the net and serve the ball into court using almost any grip, and if that is all your peak ambition amounts to, you are wasting your time reading tennis instruction books. The instinctive thing for a beginner is to grab the racket in that well-known "shake hands with the racket" Eastern grip and flail away. Actually, the Eastern grip, which most players find best for their forehands, can be used effectively for a simple, uncomplicated flat serve, but it's a poor idea to employ it.

The reason is that it has become well-established among all good players that, since establishing uniformity and rhythm is so important on service, the elimination of having to change grips from one type of serve to another is vital. The grip that works for all serves, be they any of the three basic ones—flat, slice, or twist—is either the backhand grip or the Continental, and the latter is so close to the full backhand that many fine players use it for ground-stroke backhands. The Continental, as a matter of fact, is so versatile a grip that it can be used for any stroke, including the forehand drive, and it is a first-rate grip for volleying off either flank.

You may well inquire, if you don't know, why anyone uses any other grip ever if the Continental is so good and

The Eastern grip.   The Continental grip.   The Backhand grip.

so all-embracing? The answer is that some fine players do indeed use nothing else, but Utopia invariably has a catch attached to it. You can't hit as powerful a forehand drive with a Continental grip as with the Eastern or Western*; you can't hit quite as powerful a backhand with a Continental as with a full backhand grip. However, one truth remains uncontested, and since it is the subject of this particular book it is all that matters here. The Continental grip (or *maybe* the full backhand grip if it happens to

---

* Although the Western grip is used by the occasional player, notably Bjorn Borg and Harold Solomon today, and "Little Bill" Johnston in a bygone era, it is a grip whose sole function is for forehand strokes. You would not employ it for the backhand or the serve unless you are a more talented contortionist than you are a tennis player, since it involves turning your hand clockwise to the right and more *under* the handle than the Eastern grip. This way lies madness.

suit your style better) is undeniably the best grip for serving.

What is this Continental grip? It is almost, but not quite the backhand grip. You hold the racket out in front of you with your left hand, edge up, with the racket face perpendicular to the ground. Now, instead of "shaking hands with the racket" (as in the Eastern grip), simply grasp the handle from the top with your right hand, just as if you were taking hold of a hammer.

Eureka! You are holding the racket in a Continental grip! The heel under the thumb of your right hand is on the top panel of the eight paneled surfaces that constitute the handle, your thumb goes right around it to the left, and your forefinger extends diagonally up fully and then curls around the handle to the right and underneath it. Its knuckle is on the right bevel, and its tip is snugly closed over the bottom panel. (If you had the full backhand grip, your hand would be in the same general position, but one-eighth of a turn further to the left, or counterclockwise, and this too is a good serving grip.)

Why are these apparently somewhat unnatural grips the best ones for serving? You will find out as we discuss the three basic serves and the way to execute each of them. For the moment, grab that hammer and take my word for it.

Who? Me?

Yes, you. You'll have the one and only grip for the service that you will ever need, and you can forget about *that* aspect of serving. But before we get down to the actual technique of hitting the ball, there's a very vital next step to take up which you're going to execute with the other hand.

V

The Toss

The first lesson to learn about the toss is that it should not be a toss. That word carries the implication of a throw, and it also has a carefree connotation, and when serving you should neither "toss" the ball with a throwing motion or perform casually. Of all tennis techniques, the toss should most likely be the most careful, disciplined, and consistent. No one can hit a target that isn't at the point at which one intends to aim, and loose tossing produces that result. It is probably more responsible for erratic serving than any other single factor.

So what should you do? If you are a man of average height and you serve properly—which means that you're up on your toes, stretching your frame to the utmost, and reaching up as high as you can to meet the ball—the center of your racket will contact the ball at something like nine feet above the ground: If you are a woman of average height, it will be a few inches lower. The ideal toss obviously has to reach that height, and perhaps the veriest shade higher to be sure it's up there. But it is an error to do what seems to be the easy thing, toss the ball considerably higher, figuring you'll hit it on its descent. What you must try to do is to "feed it" right up to the point desired, so that the ball "sits up there" for a moment between its ascent and its fall. This is done by raising

The peak of the toss.

your extended tossing arm at the same time as you go into your weight shift and backswing with the racket arm (a vital communication link that is only achieved by practicing to get your serving rhythm), and then almost *pushing* the ball with your fingertips the final distance needed to get it to the desired height.

I wanted to get all those basic ideas into that last sentence because they are so linked together that they should be comprehended as a unit. However, they do require some technical elaboration. The ball is held lightly in three fingertips of the left hand: those of the thumb, the index finger, and the middle finger. The ball is well away from the palm, which is where the second ball is nestled, assuming you choose to hold two balls, and that ball is secured in the palm by the ring and little fingers. As for the raising of the extended tossing arm, remember that your original stance has turned your left side toward the net, so you are bringing your left arm up the left side of your body, and forward in front of the base line, just at the moment that you are shifting your weight from your left foot back to your right one. Your hand finishes as if you intended to point to something in the sky somewhat to the right of you, which you could see by tilting back your head comfortably from where you stand.*

* Author's note to "Who? Me?". Try reading those last two sentences over again carefully, if you find yourself floundering. They should sink in eventually. Trying to explain the toss in words only, without demonstration, is like trying to instruct someone how to put on a coat that's lying on the floor, without demonstrating how it's done. That happens to be a good parlor game itself, which you might enjoy playing with a group of tennis friends the next time it rains.

The toss would seem to be one of the more simple things to be able to achieve, but actually it's one of the hardest. Frequently, an attack of nerves, particularly in a close contest, can throw a player's toss off so abominably that his game goes to pieces. The way to make sure this will never happen to you is to practice the toss, as part of your practice of the rhythm of the serve generally. Practice it as often as you can until it becomes second nature. You can do it at home. Ideally, you would have a nine-foot ceiling, paint a spot on it, and toss and toss and toss a ball at it, trying to make the ball just kiss the spot lightly. If your ceilings are higher, you can do just about as well dangling an object from it on a cord, so that the object is nine feet from the floor. This may require putting a nail in the ceiling, and result in a subsequent divorce, but those sorts of problems belong in books about home repairs and marriage counseling. Not here.

VI

The Direction of the Toss

For most serves, a right-hander tosses the ball slightly to the right and in front of the body, so when you are practicing tosses, don't catch the ball but let it drop. If you have tossed correctly, the ball should land approximately a foot or so in front of the serving line and somewhat to the right of your front toe. This same toss, with not enough variation to matter, is used for both the flat and the slice services, which should be the meat-and-potato serves for practically all of us Who? Me? players. (The slight variation is that a toss a shade even more to the right can be helpful on the slice service.)

The toss direction is somewhat different for the twist, or "kicker" serve, and it will be taken up when we reach the discussion of that delivery, but for all of us who need to practice the toss of the ball, we'd do best to stick to mastering the art of "sitting it up there" a bit forward and to the right. The toss that is needed for the twist will come easily enough after that is achieved.

Top tournament players include every stroke in their repertoire, of course, and often employ the twist effectively, particularly on second services and in doubles. Some lesser-level players can do it well, too, and more power to them. But here is a case where you can count the author among the Who? Me?'s, for I think that for most of us it imposes an unnatural physical strain that can even be dangerous, an opinion that I'll amplify later. Besides, the different toss is a giveaway to your opponent who, if he is observant, will know a "kicker" is coming. The servers in tennis history who could deliver the twist with the same toss as the other two serves can be counted on the fingers of one badly mutilated hand. I know of only one who was famous for it, the gifted Australian who dominated the game around 1960, Neale Fraser.

VII

The Importance of a Good Toss

Once you have learned how to toss accurately and consistently, you've taken a giant step toward being able to serve well. Any reasonably proficient athletic type can be taught the swing and the hitting of the ball, for it comes naturally to everyone who knows how to throw a ball overhand. In fact, the historic technique for teaching the serve has been to give the player an old, broken racket (but no ball). Then the coach would show him that the service motion is basically exactly like throwing a ball, and have him actually let go of the handle after the moment he would have hit the (non-existent) ball and try to throw the racket itself over the net into the service box.

There are two reasons why the "toss" is in some ways a harder thing to make a part of one's established pattern than the serve itself. One is that, as explained previously, it is not really a toss, or chuck, which would be instinctive. Rather it's a raising of a moderately stiff arm finishing with a push of the fingertips. That's not at all an instinctive way of getting a ball into the air, and it has to be learned and practiced until the motion becomes a fixed groove in your serving pattern. The second reason is that of all tennis motions the toss is likely to be the one that is subject to collapse because of nerves. This isn't likely to be true of top-level players, who have integrated the tossing motion into their games as solidly as any other aspect of tennis technique, but it certainly can be true of the weekend Who? Me? player—especially under pressure. He gets the jitters, and the first place in which it shows up is his toss. He simply cannot regularly place the ball up where he wants it to be: It's too high or too low, too far off to the right or to the left. When that happens his service is wrecked, for, unlike most ball games, in a tennis serve you don't swing and hit at the ball, which might allow you to compensate for any erratic position of the ball. No. A good server tosses the ball accurately so that it will be in the exactly right spot for his swing to meet it at impact.*

Easier said than done, and when a middle-level tennis player simply *has* to serve well to win a critical game in a match, one often sees his toss go to pieces and the match go down the drain as a result. A parallel in golf is the three-foot putt that, under non-pressure conditions a golfer would hole out almost every time, but if the match depends upon it on the eighteenth green, it's a different story. Mr. Jitters comes onto the scene.

That is why regular and undoubtedly boring practice, practice, practice of the toss, until it's so ingrained that you never have to think about it, is an essential for the complete tennis player.

* Why should this comparatively unnatural technique for contacting a ball with a piece of sports equipment be true of serving in tennis? Well, for one thing the ball spends the minimum time in the air, which gives it less chance to deflect much if your toss isn't absolutely perfect, or if there's enough wind to affect it. Then, this same minimum flight makes it harder for the receiver to anticipate just how and where you intend to hit your serve. Finally, and most important, a toss directed at your swing, rather than the other way around, is the solid way of establishing a consistent, grooved pattern for the serve.

VIII

The Backswing

The toss and the backswing take place concurrently, and since the first movement of the backswing actually starts before the toss does, it might fallaciously be argued that it should have been discussed first. But only a lawyer would think of doing so, for psychologically the entire swing takes place after the toss, and realistically the critical part of it—the hit—certainly does.

You have taken your stance, looked at your opponent to see if the receiving position he has taken gives you any bright ideas about how and where to serve, bounced the ball once or twice for relaxation, and have brought both hands up about to your waist level, with your racket hand quite close to your body and the tossing hand perhaps six inches to a foot in front of it. Your left shoulder is facing the net and the service box at which you are about to shoot, your knees are slightly and comfortably bent with your weight on the front foot, you are gripping the racket with the butt end inside your palm so that no edge protrudes (in other words, not choking up on the racket), and while you are holding it firmly with a Continental or backhand grip, you are not squeezing it with grim, viselike intensity. Everything physical about you should be relaxed at this moment, even if you never let up on the keen mental concentration that a fine competitive player maintains throughout every minute of a match.

The start of the backswing.

But here, as you stand ready to serve, you're setting the stage for a smooth, flowing, accurate, rhythmic delivery that will only later explode with power into the hit, and even then with varying amounts of exertion. Right now, you're playing it cool.

Two things happen simultaneously as you start your backswing. Your weight goes to the rear solidly onto your right foot, either as the result of a simple transference of

The culmination of the backswing.

it or a more pronounced "rock," and both your arms start
into action at the same time. It's vital that the tossing
arm's motion synchronizes with the racket arm's motion.
They start moving together, and while there can be some
variation in the early stages of the action, invariably the
extended tossing arm starts moving up just fractionally
before the racket starts its upward movement. Throughout this meshed pair of movements, your weight remains

firmly back on that rear foot—just as it would be right through the complete cocking of your arm if you were throwing a ball—and all your motions have continued to be flowing and easy.

The only real physical exertion you may have tried to put into the action up to now would be the eminently desirable knees and back flex, which truly powerful servers use to an almost exaggerated degree. Almost all decent players have some sort of slight back arch on their backswings, and this is sufficient to give them a fair enough amount of power to supplement arm and wrist strength. But the really flexible tennis players, who can smoothly produce a truly beautiful back arch—such as Arthur Ashe and Virginia Wade—are among the best servers in the game largely because of that talent.*

But let Arthur and Virginia take care of themselves, and let's get back to you. At this stage, you're in almost the exact position that you would be if you were about to throw a ball a long distance. Although your feet have remained planted where they were, your body has twisted at the waist and your shoulders have turned to the right almost ninety degrees. Your right elbow is up high, away from the shoulder, and your wrist is cocked back so that the racket is in "the back-scratching position." You are coiled like a spring, and you are indeed prepared to spring into the real action.

* If you are a Who? Me? and don't have that talent, you can't force it and you shouldn't try. Many very effective servers simply toss the ball and pound or spin it into court. So long as they do that the right way, they'll get along very nicely and will never have to make the difficult decision about whether to have a slipped disc operated upon or not.

IX

The Flat Serve

Even though expert opinion is solidly agreed that the flat service is not the one to be used most of the time, I don't think there is a tennis instruction book that has ever been written that does not start out with it in describing the three types of basic serves. The Bible might just as well begin with some book other than Genesis. This tennis book isn't going to break the precedent, and it's not due to timidity. It is simply because the flat serve, being so close in its nature not only to the throwing of a ball overhand but to the driving in of a nail with a hammer, is the easiest to learn first. The other two types of services can be learned later by adding adaptations.

So the ball is in the air and you are coiled with your elbow high, your wrist cocked, and your racket back, poised for a second before the moment of truth.

Just as in the throwing of a baseball, the hips and shoulders now uncoil and turn counterclockwise back toward their original positions at exactly the same moment that your weight swings forward again onto your front foot. Just as in driving in an overhead nail with a hammer, you swing up and reach to your fullest extent with your racket and throw its head at the point where the toss will meet it. All the weight of your body, leaning into the hit, is behind it, and at the moment of contact your

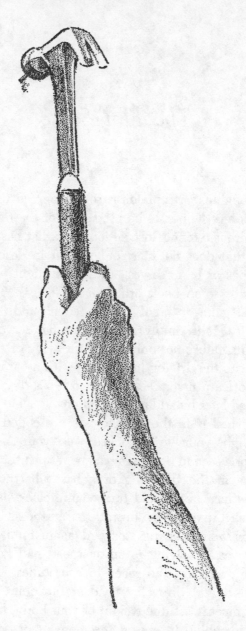

Hitting a flat serve is just like driving a nail into the wall.

legs, body, serving arm, and racket are practically in a straight line, slanting upward from behind the base line into the court. I cannot emphasize too much the necessity of getting your toss up to the right spot and stretching and reaching *up* to your fullest extent in meeting the ball, which should still be slightly in front of your head despite your leaning forward. When a person's service goes sour, invariably one of two factors causes it. The first, an erratic toss, has already been discussed. The other is failure to get that racket up to the height it should attain on a good toss. Mechanically you may think it's impossible, but you should at least have the feeling that you are not only trying to hit the ball at the highest possible point, but actually hit up and over the top of it!

The fact is that, if you uncock your wrist properly just before the hit, and whip the racket at the ball with a snap of your wrist in the forward direction, you'll be doing just that. From the back-scratching position to the moment just after the hit, your wrist uncocks so completely that the racket head moves through a full 180° arc while your arm travels only about a foot and a half! The snap of the wrist is what gives a service oomph! (A marvelous arching of the back helps a lot too, but only those favored by the gods in their physique and flexibility get that advantage.)

There is one other thing, however, which neither pros nor teaching manuals ever seem to cover, and which adds considerably to the force with which you can deliver a serve. Do you remember, when you were reading about the Stance and the Backswing, that I advised holding the handle of your racket firmly, but not in a death grip, and told you I'd explain why later? The moment has come.

The basic serving motion for the flat serve and for the slice serve is very similar, and this sequence illustrates equally well the flow of action for either type of service. The distinction between the two lies in a slightly different direction of

the lateral toss of the ball, and the way the strings of the
racket are brought into contact with the ball. These variances
are illustrated on pages 41 and 51.

Let's return to the comparable motion of using a hammer. You hold it reasonably loosely in your fingers as you start the hammering stroke. But just the split second before you actually hit the nail, not only do you get your wrist into it but your *fingers* tighten! The same is true of any such action in athletics, whether it's hitting a golf ball, throwing a ball or a javelin, or fly casting with a fishing rod. To get punch, your fingers simply must tighten at the critical moment, and for them to be able to do so, they cannot previously have been locked like a vise onto whatever they were holding.

So just as your racket arm stretches up and reaches its highest point, and your wrist uncocks in all its fury, your fingers tighten on the handle as well, and a sizzling untouchable flat serve zooms over the net, bites into the corner of your opponent's service box, and is past him for a clean ace! As you follow through and take your first step into the court, your arm sweeps down across your body to the left, with the racket finishing up on that side of your body, near your foot.

I hear a plaintive voice saying, "Who? Me?" The answer is, "Yes! You!"—but only now and then, not so much because you can't do it more often, but because it's a bad idea to try it too frequently. If you are very tall and a marvelous server to boot, you may well rely upon the flat serve more than the percentages indicate is wise, but if you are somewhat shorter and less gifted, there are better ways. The trouble with the flat serve, as your primary weapon, is a simple matter of geometry. Smashing a tennis ball full power at the height most players can attain, but having to be sure that the ball clears the net, means that too frequently it has no chance of staying within the confines of the service box at which it's aimed and sails past the line for a fault. Gravity is not enough to pull it down, so unless you are very tall and can therefore achieve a sharper angle of descent, be mighty selective about when you decide to use the all-out, full-strength flat serve. Otherwise, the percentage of them that you'll put into play successfully will not be high enough to pay off, and what is more, it's a very tiring serve to keep up through a long match.

The flat serve certainly has its important uses, particularly in singles. It wins points outright. It can intimidate an opponent. When you ace a person with one, there are few more satisfying tennis experiences. Most important, banging in a good, flat serve now and then, after sending over other slower-paced, spin services, can catch the receiver off guard and force an error. A flat serve in such circumstances, if well placed, often achieves that result even when, to play safe, the server takes a little pace off his delivery and doesn't hit out full force. Learn and use the flat serve, but pick your spots.

In doubles, the flat serve should be used even more sparingly. Getting the ball into play, getting the first service in, and practically never double-faulting, are the first credos of successful doubles play. The flat delivery is the service that most frequently will violate those tenets. Additionally, since the server in doubles wants to follow his serve in and advance to the net for a volley, a slower-paced offering gives him more time to get into position.

So, for many reasons, you had better learn at least another type of service and, with luck and talent, two others. Read on!

X

The Slice

No one has the right to call himself "a tennis player" who has not worked at mastering the slice service and obtained at least an adequate performance with it. This is the basic serve for anybody whose ambition extends past "patty-caking" a tennis ball into play on the serve, and it's also the basic serve for the top performers who play the tournament circuit. There is no other service that can be struck so well, so effectively, so consistently, and with as little strain on the physique as the slice. It is used the majority of the time as one's first serve, and very nearly all the time as one's second serve, in singles. It is almost the only serve that makes sense for most players to use in doubles.

Those are pretty sweeping statements, and they could justifiably be contested by two minority categories of players. Tall, powerful, talented servers of the flat "cannon ball" service certainly are going to use that potent weapon much more frequently on their first serves, both in singles and in doubles, than the rest of us. And those comparative few who can really master the intricacies and physical strain of the twist, or "kicker," employ it often and very effectively. But let's face it. You will hardly ever encounter a club-level weekend player who can and does. A first-rate "kicker" serve is a weapon in the armory of all world-class players and of many really top-notch performers, but it's simply beyond the capability of even a very good hacker.

That brings us back to the slice service, which should be every tennis player's best friend, be he ranked nationally or be he a Who? Me? It's easy to learn, because you start out easily and gradually, not trying to achieve too much, but merely getting to understand how it works and why it's so valuable. Then, as you gain confidence in your ability, you can build up its ramifications and play the slice with variations that range from pianissimo to fortissimo. Let's start at the beginning.

Take that box of used balls out with you one day, and set it down alongside you as you assume the same stance on the base line for serving into the deuce box as you did for the flat serve. You are going to grip the racket, go into your backswing, shift your body weight, and make your toss exactly as you've been doing when serving flat, with the only difference being that you'll direct the toss fractionally more forward and to your right. What do I mean by "fractionally"? Well in this case, if you were to let the toss for your slice fall to the ground, I'd estimate it might land as much as a foot-and-a-half in front of the serving line (rather than a foot), and perhaps half-a-foot farther out to the right of your front toe than it did on the toss for the flat. It's not very different, and once you've infused yourself with the rhythm and motion of the toss so that it's second nature, you'll have no difficulty in actually carrying out a proper toss for the slice: You just should remember to do it. A little farther forward, a little more off to the right. Easy.

This gets you to the point where you have twisted your

body to the right and are coiled, weight-on-back-leg, your elbow high and your racket cocked back in the position of momentary pause, just before you go into the actual serve. The toss is on the point of leaving your finger tips, and if you were delivering a flat serve, you'd be about to stretch up and hammer it home as if you were Thor.

Hold it! Wait a minute! You have just finished reading what's wrong with using the flat serve as a regular thing, and how it's quite more likely to go into the net or sail over the service line than zing into court. This section is supposed to be about a different serve that's just as good or better—the slice. So what do you do about that method of serving?

You take it easy. You swing your racket up with your arm in a fluid, easy, almost lazy motion, and make the racket head sweep round the outside (right side) of the ball on its way forward. The strings go into and around that outside segment in a sharp brushing motion. They don't meet the ball full face, as they do on the flat serve. This brushing motion obviously does more than propel the ball forward (it does that, too, if not as powerfully as on the flat serve)—it also imparts a strong, side-spinning motion to it. To do this effectively, you must unleash full wrist action and snap your racket face sharply half-into and half-alongside the ball, as well as up and over it on the follow-through. That wrist snap is really the only fairly strong exertion you exercise, in first learning the slice, and even it should be moderate and controlled at first.

Think of how a baseball pitcher warms up before he starts throwing hard balls. Take it easy and keep your motion as fluid and as unstrained as his. At first you may

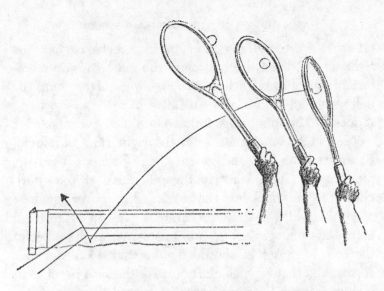

On the slice serve, the ball is tossed slightly to the right, and the face of the racket is brushed over the top right-hand "corner" of the ball to impart a clockwise spin.

hit a lot of balls erratically, because this isn't as natural as the simple flat serve act of hammering a ball straight ahead. But soon you'll begin to get the feel of what you're doing, and it will be gratifying fun. For one thing, this upward, brushing motion is going to lift the trajectory of your serve much higher than the intentionally low, line-drive path of the hard-hit flat serve, so your balls will be clearing the net comfortably instead of plunking into it. For another, the combination of sidespin (from brushing the ball) and topspin (from snapping your wrist and bringing the strings up and over the ball) will do what gravity fails to do on the flat serve. The ball will dip after it crosses the net and fall safely within the service box.

The thing to do with your box of used balls is to keep serving one ball after the other, easily and fluidly, with no attempt to do anything more than to make contact the right way and see the ball clear the net by a very comfortable margin. Note that although you might think the ball would go too far, since it sailed over the net so high, it doesn't. The spin brings it down into the service box.

Keep at it, sometimes from the right side and sometimes from the left, and when all the balls are used up, pick up your box, walk to the other end of the court, chuck the balls back into the box,* and start over again.

After a while, see how accurately you can make these lazy, easy-spin services go into one corner or the other of the box. Most serves should be directed deep and to a corner, and that is particularly true of the slice because its bounce, after hitting the court, is geared to make things uncomfortable for the receiver if it lands in a corner. We'll go into this more fully a little later on.

When you feel you have a reasonably good understanding of how this experimental, warming-up use of spin works—and gratifyingly consistent control of it—start trying some more sophisticated tricks with it. Obviously, the more sharply you have your racket strings bite into the ball in the brushing action, the more spin you will be imparting to it. The more spin you give the ball, the greater its swerve and the more pronounced its bounce, but its trajectory will be higher and its speed less than if you hit it flat or gave it only a moderate amount of slice. That sharp slicing motion is the one that you've been hitting up to now, in experimenting with your box of balls, and if you've been doing it well, it has produced any of

* Surely, using this type of service, you haven't netted any practice serves, and all the balls are at the end of the court, easy to collect? Nice work!

four effects. In the first court, serving it diagonally to the far corner of the receiver's box, it has hit, and then squirted sharply off to your left, or the receiver's right (if a receiver existed). It would have pulled him right out of court across the side line, and would have opened up great possibilities for you on your next shot, after his return. If you had alternatively placed your slice so that it landed in the corner of the service box near the center line, it would bounce in toward his body and cramp his return.

Serving in the second court, a slice that lands in the corner near center isn't as effective as the first case cited above for, while it pulls the receiver over to his right, it keeps him in good position in center court. But a good slice serve to the far corner of the ad court will cramp the backhand return that he almost has to make off it, and a cramped backhand is usually a bad backhand.

But you must not think that the slice serve can produce nothing but slow, high-trajectory balls, and that its only virtue is that it's a comparatively safe serve which takes a nasty bounce. All that is true, but you can hit a very fast serve with a slice motion by just using less slice. You cut into that right-hand segment of the ball less sharply, and so impart less spin while hitting through it forward, a bit more like the flat serve delivery. It's still a slice serve all right, but it's something of a compromise between the full, sharp slice and a flat cannon ball. It's most effective shooting for the service box corner near the center line, in either court. A reason for this is that an opponent, after chasing your normal slice to the far side lines on several points, may leave that center line comparatively open. You may even ace him with a fast slice serve that practically nips the center line. If you ask whether a flat serve wouldn't be even better in that circumstance, the answer is, "Yes," but only if you are pretty sure you can do it. The reason for perhaps preferring the fast slice to the flat serve is that it *is* a slice, after all, if not a pronounced one, and should carry enough spin to help keep it from going too far and sailing out of the box, while not appreciably slowing up the pace a flat serve might have.

The degree of slice you put into the stroke is what I was referring to when writing of more sophisticated variations that can be learned. But the first and basic technique is to get the easy, fluid, slow, full-spinning slice into your repertoire, so that you can depend upon it not to let you down. When you do, you'll know that you're most unlikely to double fault if you require a second serve; you'll not have to poop up a patsy in order to play safe on a second serve; and you'll own the best service there is for playing doubles. Go ahead and learn the subtleties of the fast slice and moderately paced slices in between the two extremes, but they are merely the icing on the cake. The cake itself is the leisurely, accurate, full slice, and one of its beauties is you can do it all day long without tiring.

XI

The Twist or "Kicker"

Now we move on to the last of the three basic serves, the American twist, which is also known as the kick service or "kicker." In previous passages in this book I have been perhaps unduly alarming about this particular stroke, and I'm not going to recant in so far as any player is concerned who doesn't really have pretty high tournament aspirations. I simply do not believe that, for players whose levels range between beginner up even to advanced club-team proficiency, the physical disadvantages of the twist are worth the possible gains. It's certainly not a stroke for Who? Me? Even if its use doesn't eventually send him off to the hospital or at least to the orthopedist (and it well may), he'll never really get good enough at it to make it worth while. So what's the point, when there are a couple of other fine services available?

I speak from grim experience. For many years a really pretty good college and club player, I once thought I might move another full step up the ladder toward sports-page headlines if I learned the twist. I did learn it, and I used it for the better part of one season, but only with indifferent results, since I am no Nureyev and I never could achieve the full backward body arch that is so vital to this serve's really effective delivery. Lucky me! I never got sacroiliac trouble.

The twist service is a wonderful addition to your armament of weapons if you have the physique and the talent to employ it effectively.

But what I did pick up was a really dreadful case of tennis elbow, that forced me to quit the game for almost half a year. For in trying to compensate for the extra snap that I couldn't obtain, because my back was about as flexible as a railroad tie, I threw everything into my arm motion. And the arm motion on the kicker is not at all a natural one, such as you use in throwing a ball. You don't haul back and use a forward throwing motion, as you do on both the flat and slice services. No, you arch back and then snap your elbow in a direction that throws your forearm violently up and off to the right, accompanied by an exaggerated wrist snap that puts a strain on every sinew in your arm right down to the elbow.

After some weeks of this, I awoke one day to find I could neither turn a doorknob with my right hand nor lift a pot off a stove. I knew what was wrong, even though I had never experienced it before over many years of play, but then I had never before seriously tried to incorporate the twist into my game. I had developed tennis elbow.

That afternoon I was ushered into the presence of the greatest bone specialist on Park Avenue. I could not use a pen to fill out his forms and questionnaires about my grandparents, parents, education, childhood diseases, et cetera, et cetera, so his secretary did it for me, and I finally was given a series of X rays. As I bitterly recall the bill he sent me, the specialist may also have decided to give me a cardiogram test and possibly he performed an appendectomy. It was all a blur, but after an hour of this (on top of the hour I had waited past my appointment time), he pronounced his diagnosis. He said, "Young man, you have tennis elbow."

The cure was pretty radical. It was to lay off tennis for half a year. I will say that this treatment worked and I've never had tennis elbow again, but then I've never taken up trying to serve the twist again. To do the doctor justice, he did tell me one fascinating piece of information that I had never heard before. It was hardly worth what his bill came to, but it was interesting.

"There are two occupations that are likely to produce a case of tennis elbow. One is playing tennis, and particularly with an incorrect stroke *from a medical viewpoint,* and that's what even a well-executed American twist is. Some tennis players get away with it, but many don't. The other occupation that produces many tennis elbow complainants is violin playing. That very similar and constant opening of the bent elbow *outward* to its full extent, instead of the natural direction of forward, sends me almost as many violinist patients as tennis patients."*

Let's put aside my grim forebodings for the general run of tennis hacker and accept the absolute truth that no player can ever be a complete one without knowing and being able to use every type of service, most assuredly including the kicker. Certainly he cannot attain world or national ranking unless he masters all three of the service motions, and in those leagues the kicker is by no means the least important. About as good an exponent of the twist serve as plays the game is John Newcombe, and you could hardly do better than to watch and study what he invariably does on his second serves. He seems to use the twist more than he does the slice, and particularly in dou-

* Interesting, *n'est-ce pas?* Shall we get on with learning how to serve the twist or "kicker"?

bles play. Among the women, Virginia Wade's form and technique constitutes as good a model as you are ever likely to see.

The great virtue of the kicker is that, assuming you can do it well, it's easy to control. It can be hit very hard but safely high over the net because it dips very sharply into court after passing it. When it bounces, it kicks up much higher than either of the other two serves and (when a right-hander is serving to a right-hander) to the receiver's backhand. There is no return of service that is more difficult to execute aggressively than to make one off a deep, high-bouncing ball to one's backhand. That is true for champions, and it most assuredly is for Who? Me?

In serving the twist, the toss is made almost over, and even perhaps a bit behind the server's head (instead of distinctly forward), and approximately above the *left* shoulder (as opposed to off to the right). If the toss on the serve were allowed to fall to the ground, it would land in court but very close to the line, and several inches to the left of your left foot.

The path of the racket head comes sharply up and *over* the top of the ball in a diagonal "brushing" motion, from the lower left "corner" to and over the very top right-hand "corner."† The ball must be hit *hard* on this serve to get the spin on the ball that is necessary for control and dip. You can't ease off and serve a twist lazily, as you can on a slice or even a flat serve. It simply won't work unless you give it lots of zing, via the exaggerated arch of the back, and the snap of the elbow, forearm, and wrist to carry out the action. After the impact, the fully

---

† You know what I mean by "corner" in this context. If you can think of a better word, by all means substitute it.

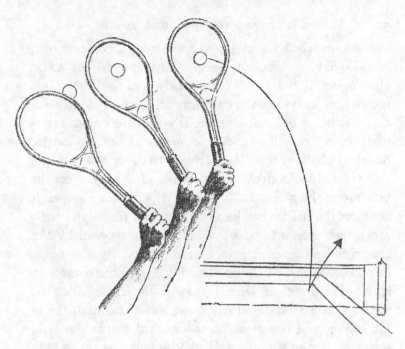

On the twist serve, the ball is tossed directly overhead and even a shade back of the head. The face of the racket comes up, through, and over the ball in a motion which, if related to the face of a clock, would be from 7 or 8 o'clock to 1 or 2 o'clock, and the finish of the stroke is up and out to the right of the body. This imparts a counterclockwise spin to the ball.

extended arm finishes the actual stroke with the hand high above your head, forward, and well to the *right* of it. The follow-through after that is little more than a return to the ready position, and unlike the follow-through on the flat and slice services, comes down the right side of the body. Your shoulders never do turn to the left, as they do on the other two serving motions, but remain facing off to the right throughout the impact and follow-through.

You not only have to be something of a contortionist, but also have an excellent sense of timing and "feel" to be able to serve the twist consistently and well. No one learns how to do it without hours of rather violent practice, but it's well worth learning if your tennis ambition is high. It isn't easy for anyone to master at first, no matter how good he is at the other strokes. In order to brush the ball the only effective way that will produce the results you are looking for, the angle of the racket face as it contacts the ball has to be very fine, and the edge of the racket just misses hitting the ball on the way up by the tiniest bit. So when a person starts practicing the twist, he's likely to spray balls erratically all over the court as a result of hitting them with the side of the frame. Even the server who has mastered the twist and has confidence in his timing will occasionally swing hard up at the ball, misjudge the hit slightly, and see the ball soar up so high and far out of court that it may fly over the opponent's backstop. To perfect the twist may require more practice than any other shot in tennis, and with all the best intentions and ambition in the world, you may not be able to accomplish it. But if you can, I know one thing about you for a certainty. You are not Who? Me? And I can suspect one other thing. You are likely to turn out to be a really fine player in your class.

XII

After the Ball Is Over

I could not resist the heading to this section, so I used it even though what I'm about to write doesn't quite apply to the moment when the serve passes over the net, but rather to that split-second moment before, just after you've sent it on its way there.

Regardless of which type of serve you have chosen to use, as you swing into the follow-through, your right foot comes off the ground and you take a step over the base line into the court. What you do after that depends.

If you are a well-conditioned, good singles player, you'll be wanting to get far enough up into the court to be in a good position to take the return of service on the volley. If you're not, you'll more probably choose to stay in backcourt, waiting for an easier opportunity to go up, and in that case the one step into court has positioned you just about where you want to be. In doubles, where the idea is always to get up to the net as soon as possible, even the moderately good player will keep moving after that first step to get up nearer the service-box line. This job is easier for him than it usually would be in singles because if he's served a slow-spin ball, the way he should in doubles, he has more time.

Let your follow-through on the serve carry you past the base line into the court.

The point of this short dissertation is that the motion of the serve should carry you into court after the shot and get you started on the way to where you want to be next. Don't serve a ball and then just stand there admiring it.

XIII

Using Your Brain on the Service

The world is full of tennis players who have become very adept at the mechanical motions that go into good serving. It is sad that so many of them don't reap the full rewards of their proficiency simply because they've never thought very hard about how best to use their talent.

Let's presume that you now have learned enough about how the various serves should be delivered, and have practiced them enough, that you've really become pretty good. Far from being so shaky that you never had any confidence about even putting the ball into play, you are well past the point when you were able to do that consistently, but were not trying to achieve much of anything very positive. Now you are definitely trying to win with your serve. Either you aim to win outright with it, or force such a weak return with it that you're in command on the point.*

The intelligent server knows that the best results come from mixing the type of serves he employs. By this I am not referring to a mixture of flat, slice, and twist serves, although their selective uses have a lot to do with what I do mean. In any case, the server may not have all three types of services at his command, or he may choose only to use one or two of them throughout a match. No—what

* Yes. You have passed the Who? Me? stage.

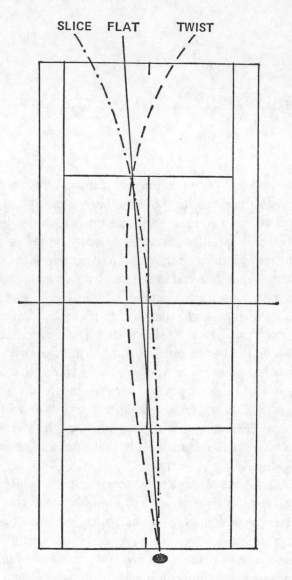

The three paths a ball takes, depending upon which type of serve has been delivered. This diagram assumes that the server is right-handed: if he were left-handed, the captions shown here as "slice" and "twist" would be reversed.

I mean by mixing the type of serve is realizing that good serving is not 100 per cent violent attack, but a judicious admixture, in close to equal parts, of speed, spin, and direction. No matter how good any type of serve may be, if it's repeated so constantly that the receiver gets used to it, he'll eventually be able to handle it and will probably ram it back down the server's throat.

The good server keeps his opponent as much off balance mentally—not knowing what to expect—as possible. In doing so he makes him commit physical errors. If a receiver with a strong forehand has lost the last couple of points in the ad court because the services to his backhand has drawn him out of court and he has been unable to cope with them, he's mentally all set to handle such a serve better the third time. He edges over a little more to his left and is ready to take the long first step in that direction. That may be the moment for the server to aim for his opponent's forehand strength, and whip one down the center line into that corner of the box. In the deuce court, the same server may have been trying to exploit his opponent's backhand weakness by serving flat down the center line. A splendid variation after a couple of those is a slow, comparatively short, very sharply sliced angle serve that hits near the side line and bounces off toward the stands. Despite the fact that this serve does not travel fast, many a receiver, mentally prepared for another serve with pace down the center, simply does not recover quickly enough even to reach the ball with his racket.

There are an almost infinite number of ways in which a server can vary his deliveries and confuse a receiver. Serving to strength occasionally, rather than *always* pounding at a weakness, has been discussed with a couple of examples. Another effective ploy is to disregard the general rule of serving to the corners of service boxes, and now and then just aim right at a receiver's belly button. This is particularly effective against an opponent who likes to take a ball stylishly at full arm's length away from his body, but it's likely to force a cramped shot out of any receiver who doesn't expect it. Another thing that you might try now and then is to serve a soft second-serve type of ball on your first serve—it might almost be a "junk" ball (but do keep it deep or you may regret it!) An opponent tuned to speed on your serve is very likely to commit an error, at least at club-level play.

A whole long chapter could be written about playing to the score in tennis, and a good portion of it would be devoted to when to go for broke on your serve, and when not to. This subject is only a matter of opinion, but for what it's worth, here is mine. Don't take any reckless chance that might cause you to double-fault when you are either ahead by two points in a game or behind by two points. If you have an opponent 30–love, or 40–15, it's vital not to throw away the next point. If you win it, you have either a safe lead that should enable you to win the game almost all the time, or you actually have won it. If you lose the point through recklessness, your opponent will be within one point of you and mentally all geared to take you on the next point and tie things up: What is more, your annoyance with yourself for giving him the opportunity isn't going to make things any harder for him to do so. Conversely, if you are behind love–30 or 15–40, losing the next point needlessly will either give him an almost sure game, or actually do so. These are situations where you must serve wisely and safely, and then work your tail off trying to win the point.

If you are ahead 40–love, or behind love–40, you may well decide to go all out and try to win the next point outright with your biggest serve, even to the extent of taking a chance on your second serve. If in the first instance you lose the point, you still have a comfortable lead and have two more points to button up the game. In the second case, if things go wrong you will have lost the game, but the chances are that you would have lost it anyway.

It's awfully nice to win the first point of a game, or the next point when the score is 15–all, but the world doesn't come to an end if you don't. I'd say you can either choose to be somewhat daring in serving on those points or not, depending upon your temperament and your confidence in your serve. At 30–all or deuce, you are at a very critical point in the game, and my philosophy would be to play the next point as solidly and well as you can in an effort to be sure to win it, which means taking no unnecessary serving risks. If you win it, and it's your ad, then once again your choice of risk serve versus safe serve is debatable, and you'll make your decision according to what sort of gambler you are. But if you lose the point, and the score becomes ad-out, I think you must incline toward the conservative on the next point, and never kick away the game by double-faulting.

These are merely my opinions: They are not hard-and-fast rules, and since the idea of mixing up your strokes and strategies is a much more certain axiom, you shouldn't fall into an unthinking pattern in paying attention to what I advise. The game score in a set may make you decide to do exactly the opposite if, let us say, the score is 30–15 and you are ahead by three games, than you would do if the same 30–15 score existed and you were behind by three games. No one can lay out a fixed plan for your strategy, and if he did it would boomerang for you because a smart opponent would anticipate your moves. So all I'm trying to convey is that the brainy server keeps deciding when to do what, point after point, and doesn't just step up to the line and bang the ball.

An intelligent server also has some notions about what to do if, as happens to the best, his serve goes sour. The first thing to look for is to make sure that, in trying to achieve power, you haven't tipped over the steady base from which a solid service takes off. Are you moving your weight too early and too far onto your left foot and swinging your right foot up too soon? It will lose you some power and fractionally slow down any advance you want to make to the net, but try keeping your back toe solidly on the ground through the racket's impact into the ball on a few serves. Later, when you get your confidence back, you can edge back into your regular motion.

If you are netting your serves, you probably are not throwing the toss high enough. If correcting that doesn't do the trick, make your toss a little farther back, in addition to getting it up high.

If you are over-hitting your opponent's service box, once again make sure your toss is as high as you can handle it well, but concentrate hard on reaching up for it and coming over the top of the ball. Try making your toss a shade farther forward.

In all of these cases, the fault may be completely in your toss, and not merely in failing to get it up there to the right spot or height. You may be throwing the ball from too low down, from your chest or even lower, instead of allowing your arm to climb almost all the way up before "sitting it up there." The shorter the toss, the less erratic it will be, and an erratic toss may be your entire trouble.

Many players are completely thrown off on their serve by weather conditions. They shouldn't be if they think that tenniswise they are as intelligent, or more so than their opponents. When you're playing in a high wind, for example, your opponent has the same problems you have, and if you concentrate better on overcoming adverse weather conditions than he does, it will give you a positive advantage. Think of which way the wind is blowing and adjust your toss slightly to compensate for it. Learn from your first serve, if it doesn't go in, how to adjust for your second. If the wind is cross-court, generally direct your serve so that the wind will help keep it in court (but, on the theory of mixing it up, don't *always* choose the obvious angle). If the wind is swirling around and there's no predicting which way it will blow from moment to moment, simply concentrate better than your rival does. But in this case, don't try to figure out the percentages on every serve, for that is almost sure to make you play conservative patsy-ball tennis, and you will lose the advantage of whatever strengths you possess. Simply concentrate hard, give yourself a somewhat safer margin in shooting for the lines, and play your regular game.

If the sun is intense and in your face when serving, adjust your stance away from it so that your toss won't rise into the glare. It is better to decide to hit a type serve that you wouldn't normally select, but one where you can see the ball, than try to combat a blinding glare. The difference between a toss well off to the right, and one over your left shoulder, is significant enough that one or the other should enable you to escape tossing the ball right up into the path between the sun and your eyes.† Some people find sunglasses helpful, but I am not one of them. However, a sun visor can have its uses.

In a long match, who is more tired, you or your opponent? If he is, don't give him any rest. Get your first serve in so that he doesn't have even a temporary respite, and make him play points. On the other hand, if you're the one with your tongue hanging out, it's probably a good idea to summon your final reserves and go all out to get the points over with as quickly as possible, and that means serving hard.

† I've seen some Who? Me?'s serve underhand under such conditions, to the accompaniment of jeers and laughter. Here is a comforting piece of history for them. Betty Nuthall was a charming British girl who, in her early teens, was too short to serve overhead effectively. In 1927 she went to the finals of the United States Womens Championships at Forest Hills serving underhand! She lost to Helen Wills in that final, but won the Championship in 1930, when Wills wasn't a contestant, and won the doubles too with Sarah Palfrey. By that time she had grown, and was serving overhead, but that's incidental to the astonishing point that in 1927 she served underhand and nevertheless could beat all the best women in the world, except Miss Wills.

XIV

Benediction

The initial first and great commandment of serving a tennis ball is to make it *clear the net*. Obviously, in the course of a match some serves will catch the net, particularly when you're trying to whip over a hard, flat service. But always in practice (and you are going to take out that box of old tennis balls and practice, aren't you?), think most intently about having the ball clear the net comfortably. From the very beginning this means that you'll be concentrating most upon putting spin on the ball with fluid, easy strokes and then, when you've gotten the "feel," work into adding more pace and direction. But your primary consideration constantly should be to clear the net. You always have a chance to win the point if you do, even when your nerves go and you resort to pooping in a gentle cripple of a serve, but you're never going to win a point when you've netted the ball and committed a double fault. No way.

The final first and great commandment is, on as many occasions as you possibly can, *get your first service into play*. There are a number of reasons why it's all-important to winning tennis. You are not faced with the necessity of having to make your second service good, which so often results in your pooping up that cripple. Your opponent, who will stay a respectful distance back in order to be able to handle your aggressive first ball, will move up and take over the controls if you're forced to serve a substantially weaker second ball. To avoid this, it's vital to be able to deliver a good, deep, safe second serve, but the best solution is to get your first serve in and not have to serve the second ball. This commandment of "first one in" is important in singles, but it is absolute gospel in doubles play. In that game, with your partner at net, you expose him to a murderous return off any weak second service you send over, whereas an effective first serve often elicits a return that your partner can put away. Teach yourself in those long practice sessions to be able to serve a deep, reliable second-service type of ball, not only so that you can fall back on it with confidence when you have to serve twice, but, equally important, because your first serve can only be as strong and risk-taking as your confidence in your consistent second serve allows it to be.

Your serve. Play!

THE OVERHEAD SMASH

I

The Origin of the Smash

There can be no realistic analysis of the smash without first taking a look at what gives rise to it during a tennis match. Almost all tennis instruction books say that the overhead smash is just like the serve, but that is only a half-truth. The action, it is true, is quite like that of a flat serve, but there are many differences, and the brilliant server sometimes doesn't turn out to be the excellent smasher. The main difference is that the serve, as has been pointed out, is the one stroke in tennis that a player controls all by himself: The overhead smash is used as a counter to a certain shot that one's opponent aims at you in as subtle and difficult a way as he can, the lob. Let's examine the reasons lobs are hit, and the various forms they take, before going into your counteroffensive to them, the overhead smash.

The only consistent thing about a lob is that it is hit more or less high into the air and not, like other tennis strokes, on a very low trajectory that almost parallels the ground before it descends. The lob is hit in a number of ways and for varying reasons, and the shot can range from a desperate, defensive, short, weak poke that your Grandaunt Clara could put away for a winner, to a highly sophisticated, low topspin roll lob over a net player's head, that is virtually unanswerable. It can, therefore, be a defensive shot or an offensive one, and it can land anywhere at all in your court, according to your opponent's skills or lack of them.

But here's the thing of it. With practically no exception, any and all lobs—good and bad—are supposed to be the signal for any good tennis player to smack his lips, mutter his thanks to the gods that be, and either win the point outright with an overhead smash, or else come so close to it as not to matter because the smash will have been so effective that the point will be won anyhow on the next exchange.

Now this theory is largely true among world-class players. When you see a lob go up and see Jimmy Connors or Billie Jean King hovering under it, you can give healthy odds on who's going to win this particular point. It takes a *perfect* lob to confound great smashers like them and send them scurrying back to the base line to try to do their best with it. Unless the lob is perfect, almost every time they can pound the ball away and off at an angle that offers no chance for their opponents.*

Club-level players, and poorer than that, often don't possess reliable, hard smashes, and are prone to try to counter a lob in some other fashion. They are nervous about even attempting to hit the shot the way it should be executed, for bitter experience has taught them that they invariably net the ball, or mis-hit it on the frame, or send it flying wildly past their opponent's base line or side

---

* I am speaking here primarily of the game of singles. In doubles, where the lobber has a partner covering half the court—and the forecourt at that—the lob is an immensely effective weapon, and the smash a correspondingly weakened one. But even in doubles, the smash is the usual reply to a lob, for it can be hit so hard at such a short range that even a well-positioned opponent may not be able to handle it.

line. So they temporize and are content merely to return the lob in kind, softly, and in doing so they lose all the advantage that was in their grasp for the taking.

So learn the overhead smash. The motion itself is not hard to learn, and you already know it if you can deliver a good, flat serve. The trick that distinguishes smashing from serving is that now you're not standing still—you have to get going when a lob goes up and position yourself correctly underneath the descending ball. Even if you have a short way to go—and that's not always the case— that element of having to get in the right spot and in the right stance makes the smash a tougher shot to pull off than the flat serve, even though the motion is very close to the same. Additionally, on a lob the ball is falling a considerable distance and rather fast. It's not like placing the ball up a short distance, and slowly, on your toss. Judgment on timing comes into play much more than on the serve, and that is why there's simply no way to perfect a crushing smash without lots and lots of practice. There's a consolation in this, though.† Once you start to get onto it, and pound in a few regularly just the way you want to do it, smashing is lots of fun.

Are you game to try? Here's how.

† There's a catch in it too. To practice smashing a lob, you need someone, or something, that will lob to you. Unless you own your private robot, or have access to a tennis instruction machine that will do it, you're going to have to enlist a friend. No sweat. Simply find a friend who is looking to practice *his* smash too, and take turns switching on and off.

II

Getting into Position

The moments that pass between the second you see your opponent toss up a lob and the second you actually attempt to smash it away are actually likely to spell success or failure even more than how brilliantly you do, or do not, hit the shot. By this I mean that something short of perfection on the execution of the smash—and this even includes a grievous mis-hit such as hitting off the wood or metal frame—has a chance of being a winner. Usually your opponent is deep in his court, hoping rather helplessly that he'll be able to scramble and at least have a chance of reaching your smash. If you get into position but don't bring it off well, but the ball does at least clear the net in a direction and distance that you didn't intend and he didn't expect, it may be just as effective as if you had pounded it away for a clean winner. On the other hand, it's virtually impossible to do anything but flub the ball into the net or out of court if you try to smash from anything less than the right place. If you don't believe that, just try executing a decent serve off a wild toss.

So, just as the lob is lofted up by your opponent, start your preparation to meet it. You should do three things simultaneously. Turn your body so that your left shoulder faces the net, switch to the serving grip (unless you use the Continental for all shots, which would make this un-

Start preparing as you see a lob go up.

necessary), and immediately start moving toward the place you should be so that you can effectively take the descending ball most comfortably. If you wait until it's on its way down, you're going to be too late.

Even a short and not particularly high lob gives you enough time to get to the right position if you start right away. A high lob gives you plenty of time, and you don't have to be a track star to get to where you want to be before the moment of truth. You don't even run to try to get under most lobs. Rather, with your body still in its sideways position, and whether you have to move up or back, right or left, you stay pretty solidly on the court surface and move to the right spot employing short, gliding, overlapping steps. This seems worth explaining in a little more detail, because every tennis instructional manual I've ever seen calls them "skips," which implies a bouncing motion, and which seems to me to give something of a false picture.

If, let us say, the lob is a good one and you have to move back for it, your first step would be a normal one with your right foot to the rear, with your foot not coming off the ground very far. Just as the ball of that foot connects again with the court, you half-glide, half-drag your left foot back to a point just back of where your right foot had taken off, and this is the "overlapping steps" aspect of the movement. Now you are a stride back of where you started, with your body still sideways in the same ready position. Maybe that's as far back as you have to go to be directly under the falling ball, but maybe you have to take another, or several more similar steps to get there. Anyhow, whether it's one step or half a dozen, that's the way to get into position and still maintain the proper, balanced stance that will enable you to bring off a successful smash.

If you have to move forward to smash, the same principle obtains but, of course, your left foot moves first and the trailing right foot does the overlapping glide action. Once you get the feel of how to move in this fashion and understand why it makes sense, your instinct will enable you to vary it as may be required to move sharply to the right or to the left. Speaking of this last, if you have to move to your left, keep moving! Most lobs will give you

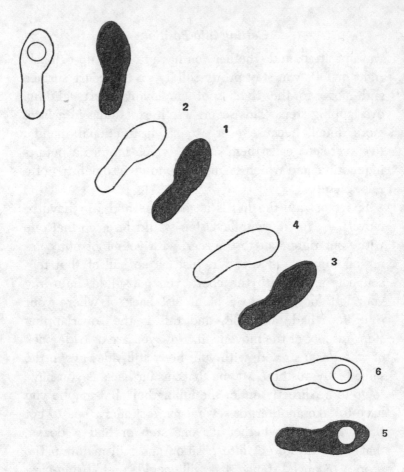

The numbers indicate the order of your backward steps. The circles indicate that you pivot on the ball of your left foot as you take your first backward step with your right foot, and once back in position to make your shot, pivot back to the left as you hit forward into the smash.

time to pass the point of descent of the falling ball, and so allow you to hit your return smash with your forehand overhead. Do it on such occasions, even if you don't normally believe in running around your backhand, for the people who can smash an overhead backhand with any power almost don't exist at anything short of top tournament caliber. (If you are one of them, I wonder if you might not be using your time better than you are in reading this book. I'd like to take a lesson from *you*.)

All right. You have moved into a good position from which to hit your overhead. If you're going to take it on the fly, which is the way the overwhelming majority of overheads should be hit, your position will be so that the ball will come down just a shade in front of your head. In other words, you position yourself so that at one point in its descent the ball will be just where you'd put it up on your serving toss.

Your technique for executing the smash will be almost the same as on a serve, but with a couple of distinct differences. A chief one that's all to your advantage is that you are invariably much farther up into the court than you are when serving, and you don't need the wind-up and other contortions that you may use to get power and lift into a serve. Just imagine how few service points you'd lose if you were allowed to serve from points ranging from a few feet in front of the base line all the way up to the net! Would you ever lose one? Well . . . hardly ever.

That's your situation in a nutshell if the ball is coming down near mid-court, or even farther up, and if you've stationed yourself well. The complication that's to your disadvantage is that you've got to judge and time your swing to meet a ball that's falling vertically fairly rapidly instead of "sitting up there" as it would be on your service toss. The way to lick that is to strip all the trimmings off your service motion, and just retain the essentials. You don't need the full backswing with the racket, you don't need the fully arched back or the arduous kicker motion. All you need do is to meet the ball squarely in the center of your racket, once again pounding it down as if it were a nail, and put it away. The more simple you keep the shot, the safer, and for a shot you're taking so close to the net, you can get all the power you need with your shoulder, elbow, and wrist.

The first simplification is to take the racket up in front of your body, instead of up behind your back. Think of just raising your right elbow up about as high as it will comfortably go, which will be almost to the top of your head. Your elbow bends sharply as it gets up there, and you cock your wrist, so that your racket drops back of your head in the back-scratching position. All this can be done easily and fluidly, without any elaborate wind-up. As you do it to counterbalance your body—just as you'd do if cocking your arm back to throw a ball a long way— you throw your left elbow and arm up and forward. The real purpose of this is for balance, but in tennis slamming there's a dividend in the gesture if you also extend your forearm and outstretched fingers toward the ball in flight and follow its descent as if you were going to catch the ball with that left hand. It keeps you side-on to the net all the way, preventing the collapse to the right that plagues so many attempted smashes, and it makes you focus hard on the falling ball throughout its descent.

Now all you have to do is to hit the ball.

There are two schools of thought about this. The one holds that you ought to jump from the balls of your feet up at the ball and hit it while you're in the air. The adherents of this viewpoint have several good arguments. Obviously, you can get up higher to take a lob that might clear

Ready to smash a lob.

your racket if your feet were on the ground. Also, since you definitely should jump for a deep lob that you have to take on the fly back near your base line (this will be explained later), they argue that you're better off to be consistent and take all overhead smashes this way. Finally, they maintain that your timing is better if you go up to meet a falling ball, than if you wait for it to reach you.

Taking off for a jump smash.

I think there's little doubt that these points are all valid, and the best players do take off into the air on smashes. So that technique gets my admiring vote, but there are sufficiently good points to be made for anchoring at least one foot on the ground—the back foot—to go into that too, and I imagine the Who? Me?'s among us will be grateful. The leaping smash does seem a little too Nijinsky-like to be something we hackers can be confident about, and most of us feel more secure, particularly in the

Smashing with the back foot anchored.

forecourt, with the right foot solidly on terra firma and a slight lifting of the left foot as we shift weight onto it and step into the smash.

When you're taking a lob in mid- to forecourt, whether you jump for it or not, there is really only one right way to hit it. BAM! You may choose the direction in which you aim it, depending upon where your opponent isn't or isn't likely to be, but the actual hit itself should be all out and never timid. If in your preparation you have held your right elbow high (this is the most important thing to concentrate upon, because it *makes* you reach up to the limit in throwing your racket at the ball), and if your elbow and wrist are cocked, all you need do is to whack the ball in a simplified shorter flat-service style. Drive that nail home! Slice and spin are both unnecessary, and they're likely to produce unnecessary errors. Just aim at a spot and carry through as if you were throwing the racket itself right over the net at it.

Playing up this close to the net for the smash if you meet the ball squarely and take it at the top of your reach, you won't be netting any smashes. If anything, you may hit too far and out of court. Here's a little tip that can prevent that. If you make sure that at impact the head of your racket is slightly in front of your hand, and not right above it or even back of it, you've *got* to hit the ball downward and it will stay in court no matter how hard you smash it. But don't collapse on the shot—make sure you hit solidly into and over the top of the ball and follow through, just as you do on a flat serve.

Now, what if the lob that is thrown up against you is deep, and you have to go way back near your base line to take it? First, unless it's very high, you'll have to dig hard with those overlapping step-glides to get back in time, but it usually can be done, and let's say you've done it.*

* If you haven't, you're going to have to scramble and try to get the ball back somehow with a shot that certainly won't be a smash. This book is limited in its subjects, and isn't supposed to cover that. But lots of luck to you!

Now you really have to jump off your back foot to make any overhead that's going to be effective, since you need extra height both to clear the net and to increase the angle that now has become much tougher than when you were up in the forecourt. The illustration on page 76 shows this change in circumstances vividly.

To make this jump, you have to lean back on your rear (right) foot and take off from the ball of that foot, but get both feet up. As you swing back, and even up into impact with your racket, your body is actually inclined backward in mid-air. You regain your balance by landing on your left foot just after impact, while your right foot swings forward and keeps you on keel.

You may have noticed that I've shifted away from the word "smash" since I started discussing these deep ones, and have turned to "overhead." That's because while you may decide to smash such lobs full strength—and there are indeed occasions where its the best idea—there probably are even more occasions, particularly in doubles, when hitting a deep overhead at half- or three-quarters speed to the right spot is a better idea. It is quite hard even to clear the net on a conventional smash from the deep court, if you bang away at it full tilt, and your opponent (or particularly your two opponents in doubles) may well be in perfect position to cut it off. A controlled overhead that's directed high and deep into the other court, probably with spin and preferably to a backhand, is often the best rejoinder to your having to take a deep lob. At the same time it gives you a chance to move up again and wait for a not-so-good-lob next time.

III

Should a Lob Ever Be
Taken on the Bounce?

Yes, certainly, but only in that minority of cases where it's clearly to your advantage to do so. An extremely high lob, for example, falls fast almost vertically, and the timing required to smash it effectively can be difficult for the best of players. So let it bounce and then whip into it on its next, shorter, slower descent in just the same way that you would have if you had taken it on the fly.

There are two things to watch out for in smashing a ball that has bounced. The first is that it looks so easy to do that you may relax your normal smashing technique, and let the ball drop too far. Fatal! Hit it just the way you would on the fly—high up and reaching for it. The second is standing too far back of a lob that you're going to let bounce. The trajectory of a lob is such that its bounce is very close to directly up from the point on which it landed. So stand fairly near that spot so you can easily move in right under the ball as it descends the second time.

But as a regular rule of life on a tennis court, don't let many lobs bounce. Hitting lobs on the fly gives you a tempo advantage that's lost to a great extent during the waiting time while a lob falls, bounces, goes up again, and descends before you hit it. Your opponent has a chance to gauge the situation and scurry to the most logical spot to defend, so try not to give him the chance.

IV

The Backhand Smash

As pointed out earlier, if you can avoid smashing backhand, by all means do so. On a lob to your backhand side, try to get over far enough so that you can take it on your forehand. Few people have either the talent or the strength of wrist to be decisive on a backhand overhead. Most Who? Me?'s, put in the situation where they have to hit the ball that way, feel they've done well if they just block the shot back in any style, and they probably have done well.

But if your goal is higher than that, and you're presented with a low lob that you simply haven't time to get around to take on the forehand, the first thing to do is to exaggerate the turn of your right shoulder, as you pivot your body to the left and take the racket back in preparation for the shot. You need all the hitting area you can achieve in order to execute the stroke. It's hard to get much power into a high backhand, but a firm wrist with as much snap as you can give it at the moment of impact helps. On the whole, you cannot count upon putting the ball away with a backhand smash, so you do well to try to direct the ball to the most difficult spot for your opponent to handle aggressively, and then hope you'll have a better chance for a decisive winning shot on his return. In this case you use wrist action for direction rather than power.

Smashing a high backhand well (as on the left) is perhaps the hardest shot in tennis. Most Who? Me?'s will settle happily if we execute a successful defensive shot that keeps the point going (as on the right).

V

Should You Ever Smash on the Run?

For all practical purposes, no, never. I know that both you and I have more than once seen one of the world's greatest players almost miraculously dash back to his base line, chasing a perfect lob that has sailed over his head, and unbelievably turn in flight, go up into the air, and paste back a smash for a clean winner. That's just about the only time a smash is ever hit without real preparation, and even on those occasions these great athletes somehow or other manage to whip around into smashing position at the last second. They are not really hitting a smash on the run.

If any serious club player had a lob like that hit over his head, I hope he'd chase it back too. But his expectation would almost surely only be that he had a chance to catch up to it and be able to return it somehow, probably with a lob of his own. Even as you and I.

But what if an opponent's return comes floating back high over the net much like a low lob, which indeed it may have been intended to be, and not too deep but so far off to one side or the other of the court that you can't get under it for a smash? You can try something else that isn't a smash and isn't hit like one, but can produce almost the exact same result.

If it's off to your right on your forehand side, you can run at it and, instead of trying to reach up and hit it when

The high drive volley.

it's really high, let it settle somewhere between head and shoulder height and then punch it away with a high drive volley. This takes good timing, but it can be as wicked a shot as a smash, particularly if you give it some topspin by hitting up and over the ball. It's possible to execute on the backhand side too, but like the backhand smash it's pretty tough to put any real pace on it unless you have an exceptional wrist, or possibly use the two-handed backhand. On that flank, if you take a ball that high, you will probably do better to punch it off at the most desirable angle, with a little undercut backspin.

VI

The Smash in Doubles

The smash is a very important shot in singles. It is all-important in the game of doubles, where the basic strategy is to get up to the net and paste a point away. A doubles team that can't smash is a doubles team without teeth.

Both partners need to possess a good smash to become any sort of outstanding team, but all other things being equal, position the superior smasher in the ad court (assuming you are both right-handers). He will not only handle the lobs that fall into his sector, but will also move over and take any lob close to the middle of the court, which otherwise his partner would have to take on his backhand.

A sharp game of doubles is perhaps the best fun that the game of tennis has to offer, and one reason is that there are so many opportunities to slam. It's by no means the hardest shot to make, but no other stroke produces the gratifying gasps from the spectators that the powerful, unreturnable smash does. It satisfies the exhibitionist in us all. Even better, it's a wonderful feeling to smash a ball beautifully past a helpless opponent. That satisfies the sadistic in us all. If you now want to satisfy the masochistic in us all, take up golf.

With the co-operation of the United States Tennis Association, Doubleday has published the following titles in this series:

SPEED, STRENGTH, AND STAMINA: Conditioning for Tennis, by Connie Haynes with Eve Kraft and John Conroy.
Detailed descriptions of exercises for tennis players and suggestions for keeping in shape.

TACTICS IN WOMEN'S SINGLES, DOUBLES, AND MIXED DOUBLES, by Rex Lardner.
A book for women tennis players, with specific suggestions for taking advantage of opponents' weaknesses.

SINISTER TENNIS, by Peter Schwed.
How to play against left-handers, and also with left-handers as doubles partners.

RETURNING THE SERVE INTELLIGENTLY, by Sterling Lord.
How you can reduce errors, minimize the server's advantage, and launch your own attack.

COVERING THE COURT, by Edward T. Chase.
How to be a winning court coverer and keep maximum pressure on your opponent.

THE SERVE AND THE OVERHEAD SMASH, by Peter Schwed.
How the intermediate player can best hit the big shots.

The following titles are in preparation:
FINDING AND EXPLOITING YOUR OPPONENT'S WEAKNESSES
THE HALF-VOLLEY AND THE VOLLEY
GROUND STROKES
THE TENNIS PLAYER'S DIET AND FITNESS BOOK
SPECIALIZATION IN SINGLES, DOUBLES, AND MIXED DOUBLES
USTA COACHES' FAVORITE DRILLS